LEAVES

For a free color catalog describing Gareth Stevens' list of high-quality books, call 1-800-341-3569 (USA) or 1-800-461-9120 (Canada).

ISBN 0-8368-1094-5

North American edition first published in 1994 by
GARETH STEVENS PUBLISHING
1555 North RiverCenter Drive, Suite 201
Milwaukee, WI 53212, USA

This edition © 1994 by Gareth Stevens, Inc. First published in Denmark by Forlaget alma in 1992 under the title *Løvfald*. Text © 1994 by William Corderoy. Illustrations © 1992 by William Corderoy.

Printed in MEXICO

3 4 5 6 7 8 9 99 98 97 96 95

LEAVES

William Corderoy

Gareth Stevens Publishing
MILWAUKEE

Once there was a very small bear.

He wasn't very old,
but he was filled with curiosity.

He wanted to know many things.

Why is the sun hot?

Why are rocks hard?

Why is the grass green?

Even the little bear's mother and father did not know.

The little bear was curious about
the trees,

and the leaves on the trees,

and the leaves falling from the trees.

He remembered that the leaves
had fallen from the trees last year,

and the year before,

and the year before that.

Every autumn when the leaves
start falling from the trees,
bears get sleepy.

They sleep until spring.

And when they wake,
all the leaves are back on the trees.

One autumn, the curious little bear asked his mother and father, "How do the leaves get back on the trees?"

But they were far too sleepy to answer.

So the little bear decided to stay awake
all through the winter
just to see how it happened.

But he grew very sleepy, too,
and the world turned white.

The little bear grew sleepier and sleepier
until he slept –
as he did every winter.

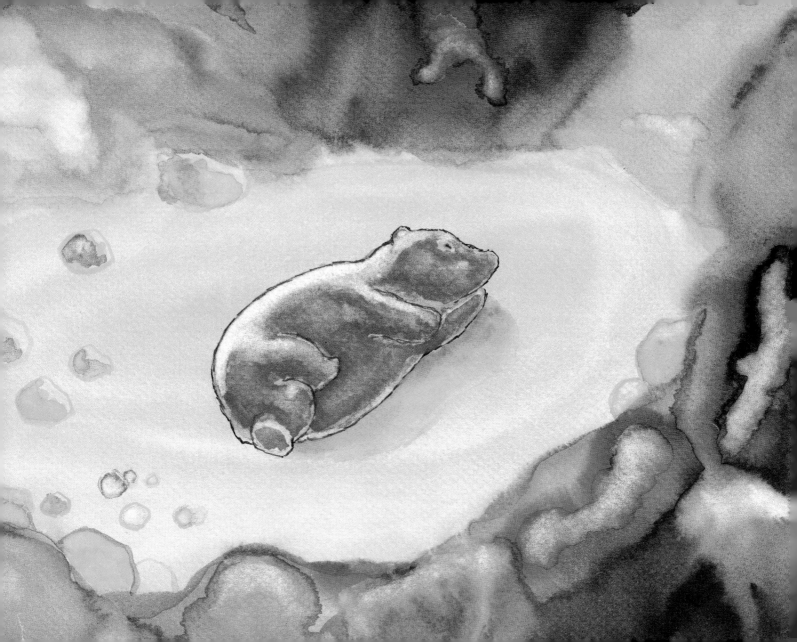

When he awoke,
all the leaves were back on the trees –
as they were every spring.

So the question remains.

And the little bear is still wondering.

Austynsal8241